REFLECTIONS ON EDUCATION IN THE THIRD WORLD

REFLECTIONS ON EDUCATION IN THE THIRD WORLD

Keith Buchanan

SPOKESMAN BOOKS

1975

Published by The Bertrand Russell Peace Foundation Limited,
Bertrand Russell House, Gamble Street, Nottingham,
NG7 4ET for *Spokesman Books*

Printed by The Russell Press Limited, Nottingham.

Contents

I

White Elephants
and
Brown Sahibs

"It is a characteristic of empires that they turn their victims into
their defenders"

E. J. Hobsbawm, *Industry and Empire*

"In exchange for a smattering of English we yielded our souls"

Renato Constantino, *Journal of Contemporary Asia*

"Soon, there'll be no Africa left: people like you, M. le Député, for
all their talk of national independence, will deliver Africa to the
West for ever"

Romain Gary, *The Roots of Heaven*

The problem of education in the Third World is, for
me, epitomised by two episodes during my period
as a university teacher in Nigeria over two decades
ago. In the first episode I was waiting, along with a
dozen African drivers and their lorries, to cross by
ferry the Kaduna River in Middle Nigeria. The
delay was long and I wandered across to an intent
group of drivers grouped in the shade of an acacia;
one of them. I discovered, could write and was
carefully outlining the letters of the alphabet in the
damp sand with a piece of twig — all the others were
falteringly following him for they were illiterate and
only the "teacher" possessed the magic key which
would open up a new world. Some months later my
wife, who had been trained as a nurse, accompanied

to the hospital a desperately injured man we had found in a smashed-up car. A group of white-coated African medical students went past and she sought their help in getting him from the ambulance. "Sorry, we're doctors" was the reply, "you'll find the orderlies over there." "Over there" was ten minutes walk away — and by the time the orderlies arrived the man was dead.

In the single-minded concentration of the extemporised literacy lesson we have exemplified the desperate hunger of so many Third World people for the education without which, they believe, individual or national progress is impossible; in the status-conscious selfishness and irresponsibility of the young medical students there is something to make us pause and ponder the social and human costs of introducing our Western system of education into an alien environment. It is with the journey between these two points — from the illiteracy of the masses to the fully-fashioned elite — that this essay is concerned. And in making this journey we may see more clearly some of the weaknesses of the education systems within our own developed societies; Gerald Hanley, in his novel *Drinkers of Darkness,* comments on the way the tropical environment exaggerates the personality traits and the weaknesses of white residents[1] — and what is true of the individuals is true also of the institutions they bring with them . . .

"A universe of radical scarcity"

The human realities of the Third World have been concisely set out by the editors of the *New Left Review;* it is an area which:

> "covers the whole of the tropical world, spans three continents, and includes the majority of mankind. It is united in its experience of

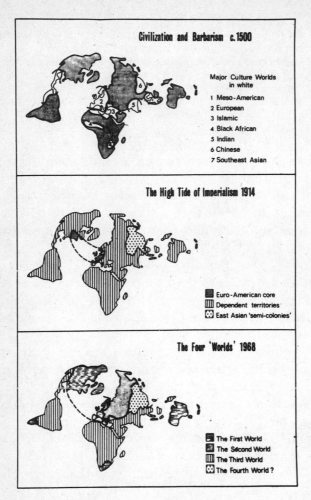

Civilization and Barbarism c. 1500

Major Culture Worlds
in white
1 Meso-American
2 European
3 Islamic
4 Black African
5 Indian
6 Chinese
7 Southeast Asian

The High Tide of Imperialism 1914

▦ Euro-American core
▥ Dependent territories
⊡ East Asian 'semi-colonies'

The Four 'Worlds' 1968

▤ The First World
▨ The Second World
▥ The Third World
⊡ The Fourth World?

1. The Four Worlds

Showing the major culture-worlds at the beginning of the great period of European expansion; the high tide of imperialism, with most of the world constituting dependent territories of the developed Euro-American core; and the four worlds of 1970 which have resulted from the breaking away of the Soviet-bloc countries (beginning in 1917) and the subsequent split within the socialist camp. It is chiefly in the Fourth World — in the socialist countries of East Asia and in Cuba — that the most striking break with traditional education systems has been made.

9

imperialism, which produced ultimates in poverty and degradation. Its condition cannot adequately be described in the polite euphemism 'under-development'; only a real use of the socialist concept of scarcity can describe or explain it. The Third World is a universe of radical scarcity. Defining and determining every dimension of men's relationships to each other . . . the inadequacy of the means of livelihood to the living is the first and distinguishing truth of this area. Pauperization is the next . . ."[2]

It is into this impoverished — and, in spite of the Decade of Development, increasingly impoverished — world that the costly and capital-intensive education systems of the White North have been introduced. And the problems which result are illustrated by the facts that it costs more to educate a secondary school pupil in Brazil than it does in Britain — but Britain's per caput GNP is four times that of Brazil; that the cost per student of university education in Iran is seven-tenths the cost in the USA while the American per caput GNP is twenty-five times that of Iran.[3]

The heavy emphasis on education in the countries of the Third World has various explanations. Partly, it is a manifestation of what has been termed the "revolution of equality" through which the majority of formerly colonial territories are passing. The "equality" at stake is not personal equality within the new nations — which would involve a disturbing social revolution — but equality on the international level. The new nations are attempting to assert their equality vis-à-vis the developed nations of the White North — and this is in terms of a scale of values taken over from the developed nations. The symbols of equality then become jet fighters and modern armies, multi-storeyed glass and concrete city centres and extravagant motorways, Western patterns of education and palatial university campuses. In part, the emphasis on education derives from the belief, fondly cherished in Western societies, that formal and organized schooling provides a means for the poor to "elevate" themselves; education, which in developed societies is seen as a means of qualifying for higher status and higher pay, is seen in the countries of the Third World as "an escape route from the bush". That this is partly a myth is irrelevant; this mystique of schooling has been successfully "sold" throughout the Third World. And more recently a new argument for heavy public investment in education has rested on the sedulously propagated theory that increased schooling of the population "contributes to the nation's economic growth and improves income distribution".[4]

To countries which are poor and within which various classes hope to appropriate a larger share of the larger cake which economic progress should make possible this argument has an irresistible fascination. That the level of education which was adequate to the needs of the West when it began its major period of economic development in the nineteenth century is quite inadequate to meet the needs of modern industry, that what Le Thanh Khoi terms the "technological threshold" is now much higher, the far-reaching implications of all this are conveniently overlooked. And, as the African lorry-drivers beside the Kaduna River demonstrate, to these more or less explicit arguments must be added the deepseated belief of the masses that only formal education will enable them to emerge from the twilight world of the illiterate.

That the majority of these Third World countries should have opted for some variant of the Western educational model is scarcely surprising. Most were colonial dependencies and under colonial conditions

11

education along the lines of the metropolitan country was essential for entry into the lower echelons of the colonial administration or into business. Most have been conditioned to believe that the Western Way of Life represents the highest human achievement — and this Way of Life embraces not only fast cars and Frigidaires, air conditioned homes and hard liquor but also a particular form of education. Few have any experience or awareness of the human inadequacies of Western life styles or Western educational methods.[5] Most have been the target of educational aid programmes designed in part at least to create a market for the new "technologies of education" being so profitably developed by the giant corporations which dominate the "knowledge industry".[6]

The thesis of this essay is that Western educational models are not only irrelevant to the real needs of the Third World but constitute a crippling burden, comparable to those white elephants which the Kings of Thailand were reputed to bestow on difficult courtiers and whose upkeep ruined the recipient. The thesis is that education on Western lines, like Western-inspired development policies, perpetuates and, indeed, intensifies under-development and polarizes society; that it is, moreover, a powerful agent of cultural liquidation. And in part this is because of the role it plays in the formation of new élites, the "Brown Sahibs" as Tarzie Vittachi terms the group, who:

> "imagine that they could transform political freedom into economic reality by following the methods, manners and ways of thinking of the Pukka Sahibs"

Vittachi's analysis is concerned chiefly with the new élites of Britain's former colonies in South Asia

12

but the general picture he paints is valid, with appropriate regional nuances, for most of the Third World; only in a handful of countries has an effort been made to strike out along quite different lines and to create an educational system whose objectives and values are more congruent with the needs of Third World societies and, it may be, with those of the technologically sophisticated but morally underdeveloped societies[8] of the White North.

Point of Departure

Attempts to measure progress or backwardness, whether in the economic or the educational field, can scarcely avoid being highly subjective and all indices are inevitably influenced by ethnocentrism; they are often devised by Western experts and the norms adopted tend to be those of the affluent society. That such norms are not the only possible norms, that other societies or other times have accepted totally different criteria of wellbeing or excellence is overlooked. Yet before we attempt to evaluate levels of cultural achievement (which is partly what education in its full sense is about) we do well to bear in mind the comments of Jerome Rothenberg on primitive and archaic poetry; says Rothenberg:

> "No people today is newly born. No people has sat in sloth for the thousands of years of its history. Measure everything by the Titan rocket and the transistor radio, and the world is full of primitive peoples. But once change the unit of value to the poem or the dance-event or the dream (all clearly artifactual situations) and it becomes apparent what all those people have been doing all those years with all that time on their hands"[9]

We have no measures of the wisdom or the skills of those "primitive" education systems which have transmitted down the ages the complex oral traditions of the great majority of humankind. All

13

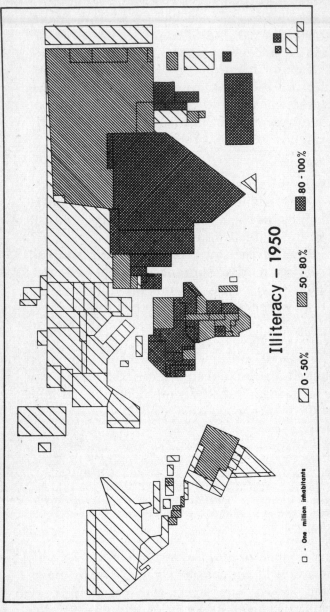

Illiteracy – 1950

☐ - One million inhabitants

| ▨ 0 - 50% | ▨ 50 - 80% | ▨ 80 - 100% |

2. **World Illiteracy at Mid-Century**

Illustrating the size of the problem in Africa and Asia. For the limitations of literacy as an educational index see p.11; for the pockets of illiteracy represented by tribal and other marginal groups in Latin America and parts of Asia, see p.13. (Data from UNESCO *World Illiteracy at Mid-Century*)

14

we can measure is the achievement of various groups in mastering the (quantifiable) skills or mimicking the educational structures of our own education system. We can measure levels of literacy, but, remembering Robin Flower's encounter with the complex oral literature of the pre-literate peasantry of Western Ireland,[10] we should not assume that these levels are more than a readily quantifiable index of achievement in one particular — and limited — type of schooling. And this same limitation applies to other indices such as enrolment ratios or the more complex and composite indices we may derive from such data.

One of the indices most widely used in the White North is the percentage of illiterates in each country. Here a useful point of departure is given by the UNESCO study *World Illiteracy at Mid-century*.[11] This suggested that some 43-45 per cent of the adult population was illiterate. The regional incidence of illiteracy is shown in Map 2, from which it is seen that, except in limited parts of Latin America and Southeast Asia, illiteracy rates in the Third World are everywhere over 50 per cent, and exceed 80 per cent in Southern Asia and much of Black Africa. Moreover, even in those parts of the Third World which have relatively low national levels of illiteracy, whole groups, such as the Andean Indians or the hill tribes of Southeast Asia, remain largely illiterate. It is scarcely necessary to stress that any real economic or social break-through is made immeasurably more difficult if to the already formidable political and economic barriers to progress are added the deadweights of illiteracy and ignorance. The transistor may, in part, play the role the broadsheet and the newspaper played in the intellectual development of the masses of the White North but the written word still plays an important role in shaping new forms of awareness, whether it be of the potentialities of new agricultural practices, the logic behind new health programmes or the creation of new social and political forms. The mass education drive thus acquires a critical importance and such drives — as in Cuba and the East Asian socialist countries — have significantly changed the regional pattern shown in Map 3. In many countries, however, the expansion of basic education has not kept pace with the growth of population; a survey of Colombia by the *Senate Foreign Relations Committee,* for example, showed that, in spite of considerable aid to education, the number of functional illiterates had increased from 5 million to more than 6 million.[12] Another, more sophisticated, index of the levels of schooling is the composite index of human resource development devised by Harbison and Myers. This index, which provides the basis for the classification of the seventy-five countries shown in Map 4, is described by its originators as

"simply the arithmetic total of (1) enrollment at the second level of education as a percentage of the age group 15 to 19, adjusted for length of schooling, and (2) enrollment at the third level of education as a percentage of the age group, multiplied by a weight of 5"[13]

This provides a rank order of the countries for which data is available:

TABLE I

Level of human resource development	Composite index		
Level I, Underdeveloped	3.0	0.3-	7.5
Level II, Partially developed	21.0	10.7-	31.2
Level III, Semi advanced	50.0	33.0-	73.8
Level IV, Advanced	115.0	77.1-	261.3

Source: Harbison and Myers, *op. cit.,* pp. 45-48.

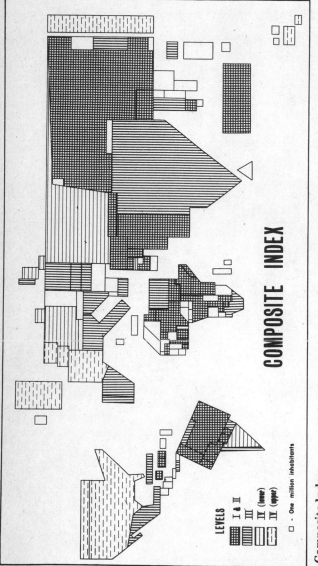

COMPOSITE INDEX

LEVELS
I & II
III
II (lower)
II (upper)

□ - One million inhabitants

3.

Composite Index

Showing what Harbison and Myers describe as "levels of human resource development." The basis of this composite index is described on p.5/6; the index provides a crude ranking of countries in terms of the effectiveness of "human resource" mobilisation. Note that data is unavailable for areas left blank and that the Harbison-Myers index, partly because of the dated quality of the statistics used, gives an unreal rating to countries such as China.

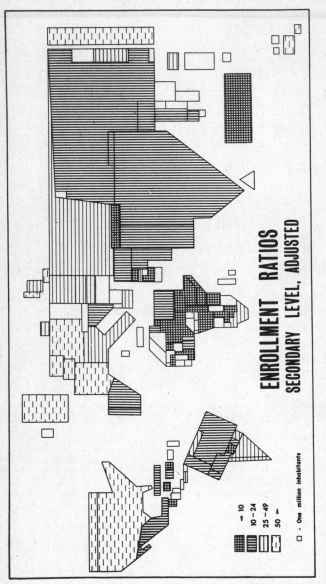

ENROLLMENT RATIOS

SECONDARY LEVEL, ADJUSTED

Enrollment Ratio

< 10
10 – 24
25 – 49
50 <

☐ - One million inhabitants

4.   **Enrollment Ratio**

The statistics on which the map is based are taken from Harbison and Myers; they refer to "Pupils enrolled at the second level of education as a percentage of the estimated population aged 15 to 19 inclusive, adjusted for the duration of school years at the second level." For much of the Third World the percentage is under 25, dropping to less than 10 per cent in Tropical Africa. Note that such statistics do not measure the proportion of pupils who complete the course.

18

As Harbison and Myers admit, any ranking such as this is bound to be arbitrary; nevertheless:

"The ranking of these countries is less significant than the characteristics of the countries in each level as a group, or than the intercorrelations between the indicators for all countries"[14]

Within the limits of the statistics available their classification appears as satisfactory as any this writer has come across and certainly there are significant correlation coefficients between the composite index and such indicators as per caput GNP, economic structure or stocks of high-level manpower.

TABLE II

Indicator	Level I	Level II	Level III	Level IV
Composite index	3	21	50	115
Per caput GNP ($US)	84	182	380	1,100
% active population in agriculture	83	65	52	23
Teachers per 10,000 population	17	38	53	80
Scientists and engineers per 10,000 population	0.6	3	25	42

Source: Harbison and Myers, op. cit., p. 38.

The extreme range of this index is from 0.3 for Niger to 261.3 for the USA i.e. in terms of human resource development as measured by this index the USA is some 860 times as developed as the poorest country for which we have data. Level IV countries *as a group* are almost 40 times as developed as Level I countries. Most of the Third World countries, as Map 3 shows, are at Levels I or II; most of the countries of the White North, with the exceptions of some in Southern or Eastern Europe are at Level IV. The gap between the Third World and the White

North can also be measured by the secondary-level enrollment ratio; this is 2.7 at Level I and 12 at Level II as compared with 59 for Level IV (USA 95.3).

These, we would repeat, are indices designed to measure levels of progress within a particular type of educational (or, better, schooling) system — that of the White North. They rest ultimately on aspects of education that are quantifiable and many Third World societies whose education system is non-quantifiable — but not necessarily inferior — make a poor showing. This must be borne in mind in an essay concerned largely with evaluating the global significance of Western educational models.

The Costs of Education

It's often tacitly assumed that, in educational matters as in economic matters, the Third World countries have to somehow rush through the "evolutionary" stages the White North has passed through in the last couple of centuries. This is quite misleading.[15] The Third World's development involves a breakthrough from backwardness not to the nineteenth century but to the twenty-first century. Nowhere is this truer than in education. Viewed simply in terms of its contribution to economic development, education in the Third World today involves the confrontation of problems quite different to those faced by the White North when it began its educational breakthrough for in Western Europe the creation of a new economy began in the eighteenth century and was already far advanced when education began to be extended to the mass of working folk in the late nineteenth century. The contrast has been explained by Paul Bairoch; says Bairoch:

20

"If, for the developed countries, economic 'take-off' could be accomplished without being handicapped by the level of illiteracy of the population, it is because totally different conditions existed at the beginning of the nineteenth century; techniques used in industry at that date were unsophisticated and based above all on simple causal relations. Today things are different, science has taken a preponderating place in technique, and, as a result, in economic life and especially in industry. It is for this reason, that the question of illiteracy today takes on a form different from that at the beginning of the nineteenth century, and this is the reason why — rightly moreover — the emphasis is today put on this problem in the developing countries."[16]

Jacques Freyssinet goes further and stresses the *increasing* relative importance of trained personnel in the production process:

"Technical progress in general tends to reduce the importance of natural resources in the combination of productive forces. More and more it is technical equipment and a highly skilled labour-force which constitute the principal element."[17]

And, he adds, "it is technical and economic progress which creates natural resources and not the other way round"[18] — which is an economist's reformulation of Carl Sauer's concept of natural resources as "cultural appraisals".

The problems which arise from the necessity of carrying through simultaneously an economic and an educational revolution are formidable enough, but they are aggravated by the fact that, in recent years, the time gap between the development of new technologies and their application has been growing progressively narrower; countries struggling to modernize are thus, to quote René Gendarme's metaphor, rather like a man running to catch a moving train,[19] for they have to move swiftly from backwardness to the assimilation of new and rapidly changing techniques . . . Yet, however poor they may be, or however great the difficulties, the developing countries simply cannot afford *not* to

21

run, not to "attempt to catch the train", not to make the sacrifices necessary to create an increasingly educated and skilled labour force. Indeed, it might be argued that, because of the conditions outlined above, investment in education has become one of the most profitable forms of investment providing for poor and densely-peopled countries one of the most accessible roads to development. It does this in three ways: by creating a "climate of growth" and fostering the basic motivations on whose presence economic development (and social development) depends; by training personnel and inculcating the competences future economic and social development will demand; and by creating a dynamic élite who can fulfill a function analogous to that of the entrepreneur in the Western capitalist system but specifically adapted to the dominant socio-economic system of the country they will serve.[20] One of the first attempts to estimate the economic value of education in a society struggling to modernize was made in the Soviet Union in 1924; there a study made by the Gosplan indicated that, while a year's apprenticeship could increase the productivity of an illiterate worker by 12-16 per cent, four years of primary study would increase his productivity by 79 per cent and nine years of study by 280 per cent.[21] The strictly economic gain is obvious — but a developing country has to confront two problems: first, the sheer magnitude of the cost of an educational programme (especially if modelled on Western lines); secondly, the time-lag between the initiation of an educational programme and the results of the programme, in the shape of qualified students and technicians — at the minimum, five years if traditional patterns of Western education are followed. The two are inter-related, since heavy

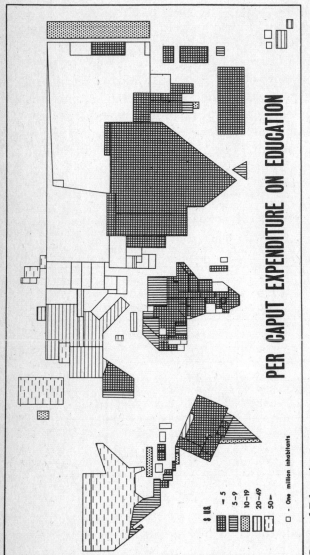

PER CAPUT EXPENDITURE ON EDUCATION

$ US
- 5
5-9
10-19
20-49
50-

 - One million inhabitants

5. Costs of Education

In some Third World countries these may represent 20-30 per cent of the budget expenditure. More significant, however, are the actual amounts spent per head of population. For much of the Third World expenditure is under US$5 as compared with an average of some $70 in the industrialised countries (USA: $151). (Data from Daniel Blot and Michel Debeauvais in *Tiers-Monde*, April-June 1965, pp. 460-462. No data for unshaded areas.)

investment in education may slow down the investment in other sectors, such as the build-up of capital equipment.

Most of the Third World countries, whose economies, in terms of productivity as measured by GNP, are almost medieval, have been sold (or their élites have been sold) the consumption patterns of the affluent nations of the White North — and this includes the costly and capital-intensive educational systems which even wealthy nations seem unable to finance adequately. The pattern of expenditure for the three levels of education is set out below:

TABLE III

Cost per pupil of the education system ($US)

	GNP	Primary	Secondary	University
USA	2,577	280	568	1,353
UK	1,189	80	128	1,180
USSR	600	87	335	1,240
Ivory Coast	—	36	425	—
Mauritania	—	76	555	—
Brazil	293	14	134	937
Chile	379	57	184	1,000
Venezuela	648	85	362	1,336
Cambodia	—	31	186	857
Iran	108	32	64	933
Thailand	96	11	42	333

Source: Nguyen Huu Chau, op. cit., p. 426.

A very crude measure of the burden of education is provided by the ratio between the cost of university training and the per caput GNP: in the USA it is 0.5:1, in Brazil 3.2:1, in Iran over 8:1. And it might be stressed that the figures in the table above are almost certainly conservative: the 1962 report on the Addis Ababa plan for African education provided the following data:

TABLE IV

**Recurrent and non-recurrent expenditure
per pupil ($US)**

	Primary Education		Secondary Education	
	Recurrent	Non-recurrent	Recurrent	Non-recurrent
Ivory Coast	49	97	324	648
Mauritania	28	57	377	753
Average for Africa	28	59	251	529

Source: Netherlands Economic Institute, *op. cit.,* p. 67.

These figures must, it should be stressed, be seen against the background of a continent whose per caput GNP is probably of the order of $100. It is not, therefore, surprising that in many African territories and many other Third World countries the education system — whose main role has been to create a highly privileged élite group — may absorb 20-30 per cent of the total budget allocations.

The situation, however, is not static; given heavy underemployment and unemployment rates, the "alternative income" of potential school-goers drops and education becomes more attractive since schooling is "an alternative to doing nothing". Initially this applies at the primary level but with increased numbers of job-seekers with primary training the acceptable minimum becomes secondary schooling and, ultimately, a university training. The economic pressure of an expanding labour force reinforces the ideological thrust towards universal education on the pattern of the affluent nations and enrollment numbers at all levels increase at a dizzying pace. The financial implications of this have been analysed by the *Netherlands Economic Institute;* their estimates, based on three alternative enrollment targets for primary education and three alternative levels of financing are set out below.

TABLE V

Estimated total educational expenditure and Domestic financial means, 1975 ($US million)

Regions	Total educational expenditure assuming primary enrolment of:			Domestic financial means		
	90%	75%	60%	5% GNP	4% GNP	3% GNP
Africa	3,400	3,150	2,890	2,430	1,950	1,460
Latin America	4,320	4,060	3,790	6,460	5,170	3,880
Asia (excluding China, Japan, India)	5,820	5,400	4,990	5,060	4,040	3,030
India	5,550	5,230	4,920	2,930	2,340	1,760

Source: Netherlands Economic Institute, *op. cit.,* p. 71.

Comments the *Institute:*

> "Under moderate assumptions the financial means of the developing regions, with the notable exception of Latin America, are insufficient to finance the estimated educational expenditure . . . The deficits are most acute for India and Africa. In these cases not even the combination of the most modest expansion of primary education and the most extreme efforts of these regions enables the gap to be bridged between means and needs."[22]

We have compared the educational model presented by the White North to the nations of the Third World to the proverbial white elephant, the gift which ruined the recipient; the data above illustrates this point. And while external aid may, to a limited degree, close the gap between means and needs such aid, as will be pointed out below, can be a powerful factor deflecting educational development — and thus social, cultural and political development — into directions more compatible with the long-term interests of the donor than those of the recipient.

The prospects for conventional education in the Third World are thus scarcely rosy; let us, before we attempt to pose an alternative road, meditate on the lessons of the past . . .

"Bitter fruit that will never ripen . . ."
Said the children of Barbiana, speaking to the teachers of Italy:

> "Schools have a single problem. The children they lose . . .
> Your 'compulsory school' loses 462,000 children per year. This being the case, the only incompetents in the matter of school are you who lose so many and don't go back to find them . . . The fruit of a selective system is a bitter fruit that will never ripen."[23]

This heavy loss of youngsters as the schooling process develops is not confined to Italy for it is one of the shames of education even in the most advanced countries. But the heavy losses in these countries become a veritable slaughter in the schooling systems of the Third World.

Rémi Van Waeyenberghe of UNESCO[24] gives us a sombre picture of the wastage and the deracination which have become the most striking features of the transplanted "schooling" systems in the Third World. "Existing systems of primary education", he comments, "are proving socially and economically fruitless for 85 per cent of the children admitted to elementary school". Primary schooling has become "the leading industry" in the countries of the Third World but "this gigantic undertaking which absorbs at least one-fifth of the national resources" has an output of which three-quarters is waste and only one-quarter finished products.

And partly this is because the primary school is concerned above all with preparing students for secondary education; it neglects first-hand study of the immediate environment and does not teach children to apply their school learning to the things of everyday life. He summarises the achievements of the existing system in the following terms:

"— 85% of children at school do not reach or do not pass beyond the primary level; 60% abandon their studies or are returned to their families; 25% finish the first cycle but are 'uprooted' by studies which do not prepare them for active life or offer any openings;

— only 15% continue their Second Degree education, of whom only 4% complete the first Cycle and 3% the second Cycle.

The output of the educational system set up since Independence no longer guarantees returns on the investments made."[25]

And, in the light of failure of all the minor reforms attempted in recent years, he concludes:

"it is necessary to seek out and find educational structures better adapted to the needs and the resources of the countries of the Third World"

Moreover not only is the system characterized by a very high rate of wastage but it is extremely uneven in its impact even within the individual country. The averages cited for any one country may conceal great contrasts within that country between the countryside and the city; in Mali, for example, three per cent only of the children in the bush areas get any education, as against 75 per cent in the capital city. Such contrasts mean the creation of new gradients, new gaps, between the rural and the urban populations and *the creation of a new educationally privileged urban élite.*[26] And, as Western-style education reaches out into the countryside, more and more children head towards school, to be trained as white-collar workers for jobs which simply do not exist at the present stage of economic development. The peasant child cannot be blamed for seizing the loudly-proclaimed advantages of education as a road towards personal advancement and, having got what education he can, he heads townwards, in most cases to join the unemployed who pile up in the shanty-towns and slums of the great cities; in Western Nigeria, for example, out of 800,000 ex-students, 650,000 were jobless.

That such a purely scholastic system which uproots and isolates youngsters from their home environment, creates in them an antipathy to manual work (and for the foreseeable future some 70 per cent or more of the population of most Third World countries will be peasants) and denies to all save a favoured 15 per cent any chance of advancement should be still acceptable presupposes

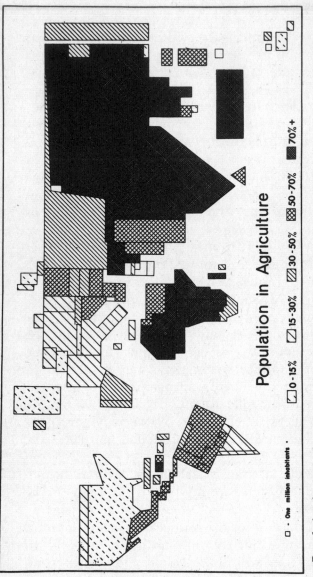

Population in Agriculture

☐ - One million inhabitants ·

☐ 0 - 15%   ☒ 15 - 30%   ▨ 30 - 50%   ▧ 50 - 70%   ■ 70% +

6. **Population in Agriculture**

The majority of the population in most Third World societies is engaged in low-productivity agriculture and this explains some of the problems of financing education. The dominantly agrarian character of these societies also has important implications when the planning of future educational programmes is under consideration.

that strong forces must support it. These forces include the socialization which schooling involves, a socialization which attempts to convice those who fall by the way that it is their fault rather than that of the system; the fact that the system is so contrived that a small group makes good and that this group "holds out hope for the large majority of the poor who fail"; and the conservatism of the teachers who, as so often is the case when limited groups derive benefit from social or political change, become fervent supporters of the new status quo and thus inhibit any profound transformation. Observes Paul Goodman "a compromised revolution tends to disrupt the tradition without achieving a new social balance".[27]

And a powerful factor making possible the continuation of what is by all criteria a Gadarene course is the educational "aid" given by the White North. Here we must recognize the role of alien education systems in controlling social change and in creating those externally-oriented élite groups essential to any policy of neo-colonial control. Indeed, as the Senegalese writer Sheikh Hamidou Kane points out, the real power of those who built the colonial empires of the Third World lay less in their guns than in the education systems they introduced:

"More effectively than the gun it makes conquest permanent. The gun coerces the body but the school bewitches the mind."[28]

And, of course, as violence began to give diminishing returns as those coerced themselves acquired guns, the weaving of "subtler nets to enmesh the new countries"[29] became increasingly profitable and important . . .

Education and Stagnation

Given existing economic trends, it has been estimated, the Third World's share of total world product will drop from 13.5 per cent in 1953 to 5.5 per cent at the end of the century. Given this prospect, the urgency of economic development is evident, if only to arrest further widening of the already scandalous disparities in our human universe. But, as Robert Heilbroner reminds us, economic development in the Third World is "not primarily an economic but a social and political process"; he continues:

> "Much of early development is, accordingly pre-economic. It is concerned with the shaping of attitudes and the creation, forcibly or otherwise, of workable institutional structures. All of this requires far-reaching social change . . ."[30]

Such social change — and it may involve "a remaking of structures" — can grow only out of the indigenous society, it cannot be superimposed from without, and it must be concerned with a solution to the problems of societies that are poor, dominantly agrarian, socially polarized and still only to a limited extent in control of their own destinies. It is against this background that the educational programmes of the past must be evaluated — and they will then be seen not only as limited in their achievement but in many respects as active agents of what Richard Hensman terms "anti-development".

Many writers on the educational systems of the White North have underlined that one of its main functions is to socialize those being schooled. The school system serves as "a control mechanism (which) helps keep the poor and the rich in their proper places during the process of economic growth".[31] It does this by using the whole schooling process as a

32

selection process, by "making schooling an important allocator of socio-economic roles" and by using the classroom as an environment in which to inculcate the establishment ideals of order and discipline. Such a process is harmful in the developed societies but is immeasurably more destructive in societies desperately seeking to break out of poverty and underdevelopment. For if the basic social transformations of which Heilbroner speaks are to be brought about, the educational system has a vital role to play, not in processing people into passive acceptance of their world as it is, but rather in transforming them into "confident and revolutionary creators of a new material environment". This issue has been clearly posed by Hensman:

> "As long as the poor everywhere hesitate through fear or sloth to cross the threshold into a revolutionary human existence their material and social environment will accordingly remain underdeveloped. It will in fact continue to be 'developed' in forms which are destructive of their humanity and their potential. The large body of tested practical knowledge, which has either been left unutilised or been used by the rich against the poor, comes into proper use only as skill and mastery in its handling are acquired by struggle. Till then it remains the hostile and hideous science and technology of impoverishment and exploitation"[32]

He adds that for the poor to ignore "what they have for generations paid dearly to learn, and to be taken in by the smooth humanitarianism of the rich, is to court disaster". And imported educational systems are an active force working against development in another way since they tend to purvey a stereotyped vision of the world in which, as in so many Western geographies and economic texts, the Third World countries are cast in the role of raw material-producing appendages of the developed

countries of the North, predestined to the poverty —
and picturesqueness — of a peasant economy.
Comments Renato Constantino:

"We never thought that we too could industrialise because in
school we were taught that we were primarily an agricultural
country by geographical location and by the innate potentiality of
our people"[33]

He is talking of the Philippines but throughout the
Third World youngsters have been subjected to this
same educational conditioning — and only a
revolution in education can destroy the fatalism such
conditioning breeds.

Imported schooling systems may be an anti-
development force in another fashion — for such
systems mean extremely costly education for a
selected few (see pages 24-27 above) at the cost of the
many, or at the cost of deflecting scarce financial
resources away from other sectors where the need for
investment is greater or the return to the community
might be very much higher. Once the acceptable
minimum level of schooling for a would-be teacher
or bureaucrat becomes the university level the
pressure for increasing expenditure on higher
education for a few becomes difficult to resist,
however irrelevant the graduates to be produced
may be to the real needs of the country. Harbison
and Meyer note that in 1962 each of the four new
universities in Nigeria were opening faculties of law
— in spite of the fact that at that date half of
Nigeria's lawyers were unemployed[34] and they
comment that in the underdeveloped nations as a
whole the nature of the incentives offered has
resulted in the proliferation of specialists, to the
neglect of the training of subprofessional and
technical personnel without whom the specialists'

work is hamstrung.

And the negative aspects (the anti-development aspects) of formal schooling with its emphasis on higher level education have been concisely dissected by Ivan Illich. Speaking of Latin America he comments:

> "Each dollar spent on schooling means more privileges for the few at the cost of the many; at best it increases the number of those who, before dropping out, have been taught that those who stay longer have earned the right to more power, wealth, and prestige"[35]

In other words, "more money for schools mean more privilege for a few at the cost of most."[36] And the anti-development effect of this is aggravated by the role school plays in inculcating the values of the consumer-oriented societies of the White North for "the amount of consumption by the college graduate sets the standard for all others".[37] In countries which can hope to begin the immensely long upward haul towards a decent society only by inculcating a new ethos of austerity it is difficult to envisage a more certain prescription for stagnation and chaos . . .

"Agents of cultural liquidation"

To give a balanced picture of the destructive impact of Western educational systems on the societies of the tricontinental South it is insufficient to emphasise merely the material impact for even more important, over the long term, has been the cultural impact. In a perceptive comment the French scholar Jacques Berque has suggested that most interpretations of the destructive effect of Western industrial civilization have tended to emphasise the process of economic exploitation associated with the system while neglecting the process of cultural liquidation which accompanied its expansion. The civilisation of the West is, he points out, truly "a civilisation of consumption", one which assimilates, consumes, all those other civilisations with which it comes into contact. It is a civilisation whose cultural imperialism manifests itself in the attitude that

"that which in the non-Western world differs from us must be attributed either to a survival from by-gone days, or to fanaticism, or even to madness"[38]

One set of values only is acceptable — the values of Western industrial society — and these values have universal validity, whether it be a question of models of economic development or of automobiles, soft drinks, housing styles or standards of feminine beauty. And nowhere is the thrust of this cultural imperialism or its results more evident than in the field of education. The very indices on which some of the maps illustrating this paper are based are the work of liberal educationists who tacitly assume that for educational development, as for economic development, there is but one possible path and that is the path pioneered by the affluent societies — and that progress can be precisely measured by the advance along this path. Reality, we have hinted, may be more complex than this and there are indeed those in the developed societies who are beginning to question the relevance of educational systems their fellow countrymen press so eagerly on those who dwell in darkness . . .[39]

Yet, as the "new élites", the Brown Sahibs,[40] of the Third World demonstrate, the salesmen of the Western Way of Education have not been without success. For it is these folk, the "Greco-latin negroes" of Sartre,[41] the "living lies" who echo imperfectly the words of London or Paris, the Southeast Asians

36

described by Richard Harris, "educated in the West . . . happier living in the West . . . (whose) opinions are a reflection of Western opinion",[42] who represent one of the firmest supports for the policies of the White North in the Third World.

They represent a group deliberately fabricated through Western education by the governing class of the metropolitan countries. They were fabricated initially to act as cogs in the administrative machines of Empire, then, as the summer-glory of imperialism waned, they were fabricated with increasing subtlety and sophistication, in either the metropolitan country or in one of the new universities which sprang up like mushrooms in the aid-warmed autumn of imperialism, that they might act as media through whom the cultural, political and economic influences of the metropolitan country might be prolonged. They were educated, are still being educated, in the language of the metropolitan power and as Pierre van den Berghe observes:

"Of all the manifestations of neo-colonialism, the cultural and linguistic one is the most insidious, the least visible, and, in the long run, the most effective . . . Linguistic imperialism is the main type of colonial influence which a former great power can afford when its cultural prestige survives its political and military might".[43]

This policy of élite-training, using a non-indigenous language to inculcate non-indigenous values, deprived the societies of the Third World of their natural leaders for, as Renato Constantino puts it, speaking of the American-dominated Philippines:

"English became the wedge that separated the Filipinos from their past and later was to separate educated Filipinos from the masses of their countrymen"[44]

At the same time, it created a docile, metropolitan-oriented élite group whose allegiance and final alienation from the masses were ensured by the excessive advantages appropriated by the group, advantages whose continuing existence has been made possible by external financial aid. It is an élite group which, especially in the countries of Africa and southern Asia, is tending to become more exclusive and more isolated from the masses, whose luxury living levels are "a perpetual incitement to the masses" and which, rather than attempting to tackle this dangerous disparity, is more likely to use its political power to increase yet further its privileges. And while this group comprises a high proportion of "cosmopolitan and polyglottal intellectuals who became bureaucrats or army officers" it includes also the teachers and the academics who transmit to the young those selfishnesses and materialistic preoccupations they acquired during *their* formation:

> "The pampered undergraduates on generous government bursaries are carefully being groomed for élite-status, and expect an upper-level position upon graduation. They remain silent in the face of despotism, but they rise up in protest when they are asked to double up in dormitories in order to make room for more students."[45]

Development in a Third World context calls for a spirit of national indepedence, based on a sensitive understanding of the nation's heritage; for an effective dialogue between summit and base, for a spirit of selflessness and self-imposed austerity among those who exercise power or influence . . . The list could be expanded[46] — but even this partial list emphasises the very limited relevance of imported education systems, and of the élites they fashion, to the needs of the "developing" countries.

"Through the looking-glass"

If educational policies in the Third World seem imperfectly tailored to meet the needs of the countries of the region they are nonetheless not without an inner logic. It is, however, a looking-glass logic, for the policies followed in so many of the countries benefit not those they are supposedly designed to benefit (i.e. the local folk) but the countries who supplied the blue-prints of the educational systems and who have subsequently supplied the experts and the financial aid needed to sustain them. The extent of the financial support needed to sustain these extravagant and irrelevant systems is evident from the estimates cited earlier (page 26) yet at the very point the bankruptcy of the systems is becoming imminent the Ford Foundation is pushing the impoverished countries of Latin American to raise per caput expenditures for "respectable" students to North American levels.[47] Observes Philip Altbach:

> "the scientific and educational gap between the advanced and the developing countries is growing. As education becomes more complex and requires larger expenditure it is often put beyond the means of some developing nations".[48]

And it is under these conditions that the political implications of educational aid begin to become transparently clear. It is true that as far back as 1960 the journal *Higher Education* suggested that:

> "There are many indications that we are beginning to use education as a principal instrument of our international objectives"[49]

but such frankness is exceptional; the real motivations behind educational aid are ususally much more discreetly veiled and the aid is "sanitized" by being proffered through the medium of one of the giant foundations.

The objectives behind policies of educational "aid" have remained remarkably constant over the centuries and, from the time of the Romans, through the Inca Empire to the heyday of the British Empire, colonial powers have sought to consolidate their position in their dependent territories by taking the clever children of the colonial upper class and moulding them in metropolitan ways and steeping them in metropolitan values. The pay-off was described by a distinguished Indian civil servant, Sir Charles Trevelyan, in 1853

> "the only means at our disposal for preventing revolution is to set the natives on a process of European improvement. They will then cease to desire and aim at independence on the old Indian footing. The national activity will be fully and harmlessly employed in acquiring and diffusing European knowledge . . ."[50]

A similar policy was adopted by General Arthur McArthur in the Philippines at the beginning of the century in recommending a large educational appropriation "primarily and exclusively as an adjunct to military operations calculated to pacify the people". Today the same motive — that of turning the victims of imperialism into its defenders, with a vested interest in the *status quo* — underlies the educational programmes of the affluent nations though the thrust of the policy is no longer towards an individual country but has become global in extent.

External aid to education, whether it takes the form of funds, educational advisors and teachers, or higher-level training in the metropolitan country, conditions the youth of the "developing" countries to repel their own liberation in many ways. Whether

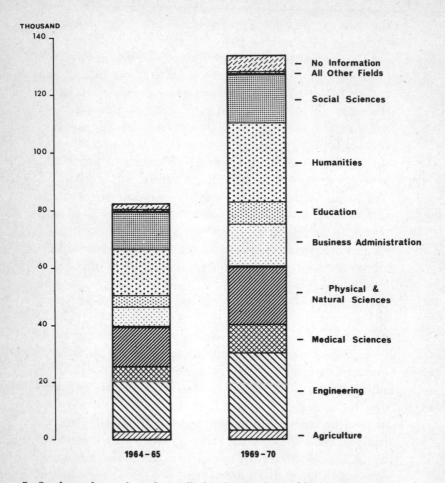

THOUSAND

- No Information
- All Other Fields
- Social Sciences
- Humanities
- Education
- Business Administration
- Physical & Natural Sciences
- Medical Sciences
- Engineering
- Agriculture

1964-65   1969-70

7. Students from abroad enrolled in institutions of higher education in the United States by major field of interest 1964/5 and 1969/70.

Three quarters of these come from the "developing nations" i.e. from countries where agriculture is predominant and where major medical problems have to be faced. But in 1969/70 almost five times as many students were studying business administration as were studying agriculture and five times as many were studying sociology and education as medicine. Given this irrelevance of educational aid programmes the importance of self-reliance (cp. China) becomes obvious. (Data from Institute of International Education *Open Doors* 1965 and 1970)

41

the aid be Western or Soviet the programmes it supports inculcate strong value orientations; the values are those of the donor nation, however irrelevant these may be to a Third World nation facing totally different issues arising out of a totally different historical experience. And these values, it has been noted, are not merely intellectual values but include the material values and aspirations of the Society of Consumption. In a sector of the world where economic progress depends on swift and drastic social change the emphasis on concepts such as "modernization" and "institution-building" means that the educational process produces technocrats obsessed with the need for a stability without which, they are taught, "normal" economic development is impossible. There is a strong emphasis on the production of elites, socialized by the pressure to conform to established (and multinational) professional norms. "Politicization" of the education system is firmly eschewed (since politicization generally implies a radical orientation) and the myth of academic objectivity[51] is sedulously fostered. And the high wastage rates of the system (see page 27 above) underline that there is little concern with the masses, with their motivation so that they might act as a decisive force for change; rather is the emphasis on training skilled personnel for private (often foreign-owned) industry or for government service. A perceptive observer has commented that many of the education programmes in the USA are:

"designed by 'experts' to 'socialize' the urban lower classes into an already existing and standardized system of education — a system traditionally controlled by the white middle class"[52]

Educational aid in the Third World has a similar objective — to fit the masses of the "developing"

42

world into an international system of super-
ordination and subordination controlled by the
nations of the White North . . . . And, just as the
great foundations are playing an increasing role in
funding educational programmes within the USA
(using such programmes as a means of cooling down
centres of growing discontent) so, too, in the Third
World do Rockefeller and Ford co-operate with US
government agencies in using education as a means
of controlling and directing social change. The
extent and the strategy of this penetration in Africa
are illustrated in Map 8; the pay-off of these policies is spelled out by the *Institute of International
Education* in the following words:

> "Us corporations . . . recognize — abroad as well as at home —
> that education offers the best means for stimulating purchasing
> power, encouraging political stability and, most important of all,
> developing a reservoir of the trained manpower so necessary to
> their overseas operations"[53]

For the advanced countries, and especially the
USA, the Third World is exploited not only as a
source of raw materials but also of those skills needed
to service the machine of Empire; it is also, and
increasingly, exploited as a source of raw data to be
synthesized and analysed in the developed societies
and which is critical to the formulation of those
policies by which Empire is consolidated and
expanded. In this field the Third World universities
and their mentors in the foundations and
government departments of the White North play an
essential role. And the importance of the links
between the centre and the dependencies is
illustrated by the fact that the US organisation
Education and World Affairs, which "provides a
master computer file on the involvement of US

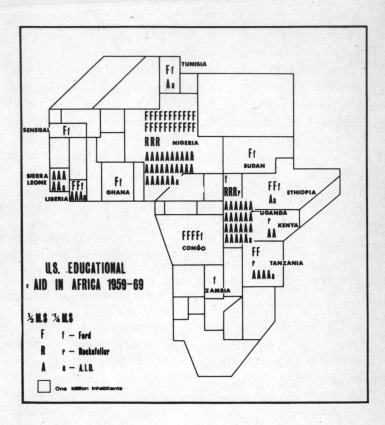

The map contains the following labels:

TUNISIA — Ff Aa

SENEGAL — Ff

NIGERIA — FFFFFFFFFFF FFFFFFFFFFF RRR AAAAAAAAAA AAAAAAAAAA AAAAAAa

SUDAN — Ff

SHERRA LEONE — AAA AAa

LIBERIA — FFf AAAa

GHANA — Ff

ETHIOPIA — FFf Aa

UGANDA — RRRr AAAAAA AAAAAA AAAAAA AAAAAa r

KENYA — P AA

CONGO — FFFFf

TANZANIA — FF r AAAAa

ZAMBIA — f

U.S. EDUCATIONAL AID IN AFRICA 1959-69

½ M.$ ¼ M.$

F f — Ford
R r — Rockefeller
A a — A.I.D.

☐ One Million Inhabitants

8.   US Educational Aid in Africa

The financial straits in which most developing countries find themselves make them particularly vulnerable to penetration by foreign governments and foreign educational foundations. This is illustrated by the US penetration of African education over the last decade. Note that the various types of intellectual colonisation being carried on at institutions within the US (e.g. training of African students, advisory work by US universities in the development of African education) are not included in this map.

44

higher education in international programmes", has processed 2,185 programmes at 522 universities.[54]

The growing opposition of the population of many countries to this cultural colonization is indicated by the claims of Latin Americans that US educational assistance programmes are nothing more than a "brain drain plot", devised to make them pay the cost of increasing the US supply of professionals and technicians.[55] And the opposition is articulated in even stronger terms by radical groups in America's oldest colony, the Philippines. "The university", says the MPKP, "is an organic part of a sick society, an arm of an exploitative neocolonial system". It is, they claim:

> "Corrupted by massive dole-outs from American foundations (and) fast becoming a service station for imperialist, economic, military, bureaucratic and ecclesiastical powers. Now fully integrated into the neocolonial system, it can offer no meaningful alternatives to the prevailing order and no original ideas for social change. This . . . is further aggravated by the consequent integration of the studentry into the service station framework"[56]

Meanwhile, the education system effectively widens the gap between the elites and the masses and between the affluent and the proletarian nations; like the existing international economic system it is a powerful agent of underdevelopment.

"In the belly of the monster"

Many of the weaknesses of Third World educational systems — their expensiveness, preoccupation with elite formation and high rates of wastage, their use by governments and other power groups as a means of inducing conformity and containing social change, their vulnerability to infiltration and manipulation by groups little concerned with education — are to be found also in the educational

REFLECTIONS ON EDUCATION IN THE THIRD WORLD

systems of the White North. The children of
Barbiana describe the Italian schooling system as "a
war against the poor"; [57] two English educationists in
their study of *Education and the Working Class*
describe the wastage of youthful potential under the
English education system and the success of the
system in fashioning "stable, often rigidly orthodox
citizens, who wish to preserve a hierarchical society
and all its institutions"; [58] American educationists
document the "increasing coporate involvement and
control" of education and the shattering
depersonalisation of Black youngsters which is
becoming the major educational problem in the
ghetto areas. [59] Yet the system grinds on relentlessly
and there is no more striking illustration of its
success in turning its victims into its defenders than
the reaction of London's middle-class suburbanites
to the student revolt at Hornsey College of Art:

> "The authorities . . . have only to stand firm. The rebellious
> students . . . have in effect lost, as their actions this week
> acknowledge . . . The system is ours. We the ordinary people, the
> nine-to-five, Monday-to-Friday, semi-detached suburban wage-
> earners, we are the system. We are not victims of it. We are not
> slaves to it, we are it. and we like it.
>
> Does any bunch of twopenny-halfpenny kids think they can turn us
> upside down? They'll learn." [60]

Clearly it is idle to expect from such status-
conscious and pseudo-privileged groups any critical
evaluation of the system. For such an evaluation we
have to turn to groups who are geographically part
of, yet socially and culturally marginal to, the
metropolitan societies of the White North. Such
groups include the Blacks, the Chicanos and other
other ethnic minorities in the USA and the
"submerged nationalities" of the nation-states of
Europe. These latter include the Celtic peoples of

the Atlantic seaboard, notably the Britons, the Irish and the Welsh, peoples who for well over a century have experienced the educational "processing" to which the peoples of the Third World are now exposed. And in the essay by the Irish nationalist leader Padraic Pearse describing the operation of the English education system in Ireland[61] we can see the emergence, two generations ago, of those simple yet versatile techniques used by the ruling groups of the White North to extend their control over their dependencies and consolidate their hold in the metropolitan country.

The English established in Ireland an education system which Pearse describes as "the most grotesque and horrible of the English inventions for the debasement of Ireland". It was a system whose products, called by courtesy men and women, were simply "Things"; men and women, he observes, "however depraved, have kindly human allegiances. But these Things have no allegiance. Like other Things, they are for sale". It was a system which made political eunuchs of many Irishmen, which made them indifferent and cruel, mere "kinless beings, who serve for pay a master they neither love nor hate". It was a system whose greatest achievement — "the most wonderful thing the English have accomplished in Ireland" — was to have so conditioned (today we would say "brainwashed") many Irishmen that they became its fervent supporters — supporters of the machinery which enslaved them . . . For a machine it was — operating with cold mechanical efficiency, processing the raw material fed into it (the children of Ireland) by the most modern methods, turning out the soul-less cogs needed by the Civil Service and the so-called liberal professions. And in this it was

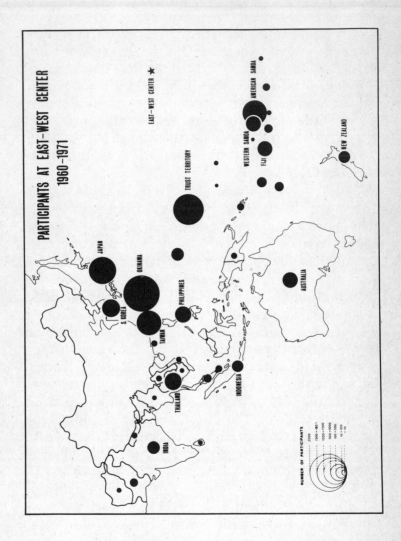

PARTICIPANTS AT EAST–WEST CENTER
1960–1971

EAST–WEST CENTER ★

JAPAN
OKINAWA
S. KOREA
TAIWAN
PHILIPPINES
TRUST TERRITORY
THAILAND
INDONESIA
INDIA
AUSTRALIA
NEW ZEALAND
WESTERN SAMOA
AMERICAN SAMOA
FIJI

NUMBER OF PARTICIPANTS

2500
1500–1801
1000–1500
500–1000
100–500
10–100
–10

9.   Participation at East-West Center 1960-1971

The East-West Center, linked with the University of Hawaii, is a major example of "cultural imperialism" in the Third World. Its programmes draw in carefully selected students from all the countries of the Pacific Rim — and as far west as Afghanistan. It meets the needs of the American Empire for the services and loyalties of the trained and domesticated Asian and Pacific middle class needed to implement the Pacific Rim strategy. Its courses run the whole range from counter-insurgent training of Indonesians to training of Melanesians as beauticians (with emphasis on hair-straightening techniques).

Says John Witeck: "The Center's past serves as its present indictment. Its future promises more of the same. Its unsavory affiliations, its acquiescence and its complicity in US foreign policy, its intimidating environment, its technological and technocratic bent, its "Free World" mythology and liberal suppositions, its elitist nature, its tourism development seminars and "modernization" conferences, and its firm stance for the status quo make the continued existence of the East-West Center intolerable. Who can estimate how many have died and suffered as an indirect or direct result of its allegiances, its training programmes, and its benevolence? Its claim to innocence and neutrality are a mockery. Its role in fostering, promoting, and institutionalizing a Pacific Rim strategy aimed at increasing US profits and control augurs disaster for the target peoples of the Pacific."

The East-West Center: An Intercult of Colonialism (Special issue of the journal *Hawaii Pono*, Honolulu, c. 1971) like the education system operated by the White North in its African and Asian colonies; in Ireland, as in the tropical dependencies of the White North, the education system "de-nationalised" the colonial subject, deflected to the needs of the colonial power the abilities of those who shoud have been the natural leaders of the colonised masses, and drove a great wedge between the rual masses and the urban elite. Such a machine, says Pearse "cannot make men; but it can break men".

It is one of the ironies of the colonial system that the techniques of manipulation and coercion used against colonial populations are, sooner or later, used by government against the people of the metropolitan country. Thus, the techniques developed in the struggle against the Vietnamese are now used by the Americans against dissident groups in their own country; the educational techniques devised by England to maintain the Irish in a dependent and exploitable status are now used to achieve a mindless conformity among the masses of England itself. For the defects, the contrived defects, of the educational system as described by Pearse are today the defects of the whole English educational programme, a programme in which there is no space for freedom and individuality, for the love of knowledge or of beauty, for heroic inspiration . . . And throughout the White North and increasingly in the Third World such a system is simply the mirror of a society which, as Paul Goodman pointed out a decade ago is "simply deficient in many of the most elementary objective opportunities and worthwhile goals that could make growing up possible".[62] In short, a good education system demands a Good Society — or at least the vision of such a Good Society . . .

10. **The Brain Drain**

The negative impact of the developed societies is illustrated by their role in drawing off skilled personnel from the developing nations. Skills, like capital, are drawn by the magnet of high financial returns and today the most powerful magnet in the educational world is the USA. One-third of the inflow of scientists into the USA over the period 1962-1966 came from the Third World.

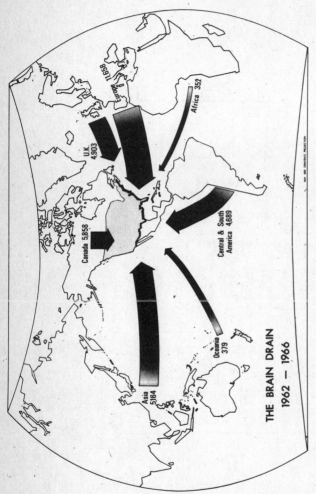

THE BRAIN DRAIN
1962 — 1966

Europe 11,658

U.K. 4,903

Canada 5,858

Africa 352

Central & South America 4,689

Asia 5,164

Oceania 379

VAN DER GRINTEN PROJECTION

11. The Size of the Problem

The increasing magnitude of the educational problem facing the Third World is demonstrated by this cartogram which shows the outcome of half a century's population growth. According to present estimates the Third World's population will increase from some 2,000 million to a probable 4,900 million by the end of the century; of these, 2,000 million will be in the under-15 age group.

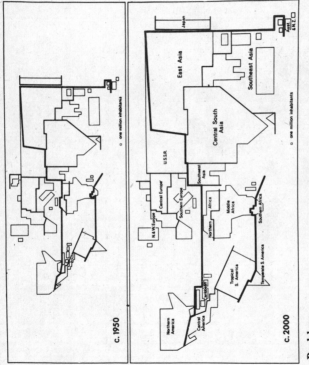

c. 1950

□ one million inhabitants

c. 2000

□ one million inhabitants

52

II

Alternative

"The vision of a Good Society . . ."
If the diagnosis above is correct the educational systems of much of the Third World are heading into an impasse; there is an increasing gap between the financial resources needed to sustain them and the funds at present available and there is a similar gap between the type of product they are fabricating and the real needs of the Third World. A drastic recasting and reorienting of the educational process is essential. And it is essential not only to the "developing" nations but also to the affluent nations; as Denis Goulet observes:

> "Perhaps the 'developed' nations must be 'saved' from meaninglessness and servitude to means by creative options yet to be made in 'underdeveloped' societies struggling to modernize in a human mode"[63]

In the affluent nations, Goulet points out, *"to be* has come to mean *to have"* and this pattern of "compulsive consumption" has, we have seen, been sold to the new elites of the Third World. Yet the aims of development must be "fullness of good rather than mere abundance of goods" and unless imposed austerity in the Third World (and such an austerity means an end to those privileged groups whose consumption patterns mean misery for the

53

masses and affluence for the few) is matched by voluntary frugality in the affluent nations all the elaborate plans of uplift for the Third World will remain no more than heartless window-dressing.

In the countries of the Third World "education" and "development" are, indeed, inseparable and the schooling system not only grows out of the vision of the Good Society but is the most powerful force in realising that vision. And any education system must confront the basic realities which the emergent nations face: that they must exist in a world dominated by technology and that this technology is a powerful agent of dehumanisation; that the process of modernization is also a process of homogenization; that the gaps between rich and poor nations and between elites and masses are widening; that political, economic and cultural domination by the White North is as powerful as ever . . .

Many of the problems confronting us arise from our preoccupation with economic development rather than with *the development of man or of man's societies*. Yet, as the Encyclical *The Great Social Problem* reminds us, development, to be authentic, "has to promote the good of every man and of the whole man".[64] And if we look at development thus we can see how much of education in the Third World has been *anti-development* — for it has benefitted only limited groups and even in the case of these groups it has done little to develop "the whole man"; rather has it inculcated those qualities most valuable — and most profitable — in the eyes of the developed nations of the North.

Education as Life
We cannot here draw up a programme for

54

educational development in the nations of the South, if only because of the immense diversity of human-kind who are citizens of this "commonwealth of poverty". But we can indicate some of the common elements in any such programme, elements which derive from the socio-economic situation in which these societies find themselves. And perhaps the most essential element in any programme is the mobilisation of the full human potential of those who have been conditioned into resignation and submission by the multiform political, social and educational pressures wielded by those in power, by the military-political-industrial-university complexes of the White North or by those local groups collaborating with these complexes. Through such a mobilisation the resigned and submissive:

"are transformed into confident and revolutionary creators of a new material environment, learning more about themselves and the earth in the course of practical struggle"[65]

In such a struggle the second major problem in educational development is inevitably posed — the necessity to break down the dichotomy between theory and practice. Learning is no longer something confined within the four walls of a classroom[66] but a continuous process, part of the everyday business of living and earning one's bread and of transforming one's social and physical environment — and as such it does not finish with schooling but extends throughout the whole of an individual's life. But the dichotomy between theory and practice is not the only dichotomy to be overcome, for one of the heritages of the White North's pattern of development and educational processing has been the sharpening of other antagonisms — between the city worker and the peasant, between the white collar polyglottal elite and the rest of society, between majority and minority cultures, between areas of development and areas of stagnation, between men and women and young and old . . . Such antagonisms have served those who would divide so that they might rule and they play a major role in perpetuating submission and underdevelopment. Yet, though sharpened by "education", they can nonetheless be attenuated and finally eliminated by an education focused on the need for integral development, concerned not with the narrow interests of a small group but with the good of every man and the whole man. And given that among the major factors in the emergence of such cleavages within society are the selfishness and status-preoccupation fostered by the system of material incentives, an alternative pattern of education has to emphasise, not competition and material rewards, but co-operation in learning and in work and the importance of moral incentives. Harbison and Meyer speak of the need for changes in incentives to attract key educational personnel[67] but it is clear that they are thinking of financial incentives. Yet additional material incentives will serve merely to polarize society still further and, given the financial resources available, are simply not practicable; in this respect as in so many other respects, the traditional market-oriented approach of the White North offers no solution to Third World problems . . . More realistic, indeed, is Castro's "I want to make the young disgusted with money". And the selflessness and service to the community which must replace material things as the main motivation for education and development will make possible the development of that sense of vocation and healthy patriotism in which Paul

Goodman sees American society so deficient. Such a healthy patriotism, involving a cherishing of cultural diversity, is in no way opposed to a vigorous spirit of internationalism; indeed, it is the only soil in which a real internationalism, as opposed to the chauvinism of many Third World elites, can grow.[68]

There are two final yet fundamental reasons why the educational models of the White North are irrelevant to the needs of the people of the Third World. First, since all the underdeveloped societies have entered, or are entering, a period of profound economic and social change and since the contours of the future are as yet vague and uncharted the need is for people trained to turn their hands — and their minds — to a wide range of occupations. The narrow specialisation increasingly characteristic of the affluent societies would be disastrous; rather is the need for versatility, for folk whose qualities are best summarised in the French term "polyvalent". Secondly, financial realities mean that the capital-intensive and expensive education systems of the North have no place in the Third World; education, if it is to be within reach of the masses, must be so organised as to be cheap, easily disseminated, and as far as is possible financially self-supporting. While the costs of job-training in the developed societies have increasingly been shifted by industry and business on to the shoulders of the taxpayer, these costs in the emerging nations will to a large extent have to be borne by the enterprise. This will mean an emphasis on on-the-job training — which will have the result of eliminating much of the irrelevant material which clutters up the syllabuses derived from the traditional schooling systems of the North. And if education is developed so as to be more self-supporting and as an integral part of economic activity the penetration and subversion of a country's educational system by external agencies operating under the cloak of "aid" are no longer possible — and a greater effective control over the system will be — indeed, must be — exercised by the local community. Which is what appears to be happening in the socialist societies of East Asia. However, since there are many who still cling to the belief that the distinguishing features of these societies is "irrationality piled on inhumanity" it should be underlined that other educationists who have examined the pathology of existing systems of schooling propose changes very similar to those the Chinese are carrying through.

Reflections from South of the Border

The irrelevance to life of much of what is taught, the use of schooling (and especially the exam system) to induce conformity and to grade and de-grade, the preoccupation of schools with elite formation, the divorce between theory and practice, the shameful wastage of young talents and of youthful idealism — all these aspects of the Western educational model have been bitterly attacked by perceptive critics in the White North.[69] But the strongest attack on the sacred cows of educational tradition has come from those who have worked as educators in the Third World and who have seen clearly the gap, the widening gap, between the reality and the myths still so industriously peddled by the majority of educationists. Outstanding among these critics are Paolo Freire and Ivan Illich, both of whom draw on their experience of Latin America.[70]

Under Third World conditions, equal schooling on obligatory lines is, says Illich bluntly:

"economically absurd, intellectually emasculating, socially polarizing and destructive of the credibility of the political system which promotes it"[71]

Education, as opposed to schooling, cannot in reality be separated from the business of day-to-day life, yet, given existing Western educational models:

"Work, leisure, politics, city living and even family life depend on schools for the habits and the knowledge they presuppose, instead of *becoming themselves the means of education*" (emphasis added)[72]

Indeed, he comes to the heart of the matter when he emphasises the dangers of the illusion that most learning is the result of teaching, when in reality most people acquire most of their knowledge outside school as a by-product of other activities. From this he moves to the idea of "skill centres" which would make possible the generalization in the community of skills already acquired by people who use them. Such centres would in many cases be attached to the work place itself, with employers and staff "supplying instruction as well as jobs to those who choose to use their educational credits this way". This means that we have to rid ourselves of the idea that "manpower qualification must precede employment, that schooling must precede productive work". Rather should training and education be on the job, with industrial plants not only offering after-work training but also redesigning the industrial process so that it has educational value. The idea of conventional adult education courses — which offer a form of compensatory training to the underprivileged for what he has somehow missed — overlooks, Illich points out, that all education is an exercise in adulthood, that the real school is, in fact, life itself. And here he comes to his most radical suggestion — that the duration of formal, obligatory, schooling should be cut to two months a year and that this type of schooling should be spread out over 20-30 years of a man's life. In-service apprenticeship and the like would provide most of what we term "instruction" and the two months each year would give leisure for the pursuit of insight — which is what the Greeks understood by "schole".[73]

When we look at some of Illich's ideas on "education", as opposed to simply learning a skill, we again find close parallels with the emerging education system of China. Education, says Illich, "relies on the relationship between partners who already have some of the keys which give access to memories stored in and by the community"; it is essentially a co-operative enterprise. Creative exploratory learning (which is just what the developing nations need most) "requires peers currently puzzled about the same terms or problems" and this leads to the idea of an alternative to the traditional school in the shape of a network or service which "gives each the same opportunity to share his current concern with others motivated by the same concern". Such a system would be very different to the competitive pattern of book-learning typical of the educational systems of the White North. Education *for* all means education *by* all; this implies that the rights to teach now monopolised by a special elite possessing the appropriate paper qualifications become everyone's rights. This would mean an end to the present situation in which the self-taught individual is regarded as of no account and would lead to the recognition that "most learning is not the result of instruction. It is rather the result of unhampered participation in a meaningful setting". Education becomes far less formal, the gap separating work and leisure is diminished, and education becomes a lifelong process, to which all experiences, all the institutions of society, contribute. And in this context he underlines the educational role of organisations such as the CCP, of guerrilla warfare in Latin America, of the teachings and actions of Catholic radicals, of the speeches of Fidel Castro. And while he recognizes the specificity of Latin American society, and that "a sweeping utopia like the Chinese commune" is scarcely applicable to the very different conditions of Latin America, he suggests that we *should*:

"plunge our imagination into the construction of scenarios which would allow a bold reallocation of educational functions among industry, politics, short scholastic retreats, and intensive preparation of parents for early childhood education"[74]

It is precisely because the Chinese are pioneering such a "bold reallocation of educational functions", and this on a subcontinental scale, that the Chinese experiment is of such critical relevance to other emerging countries.

"Every educational practice implies a concept of man and the world"[75]

The peoples of the East Asian socialist regimes — the Chinese, the Vietnamese, the Pathet Lao and the North Koreans — share a common experience of poverty, exploitation and, more recently, of massive Western aggression. Yet they are virtually alone among the formerly dependent peoples of the globe in their success in breaking the shackles which bound them and in initiating an autonomous and self-sustaining process of social and economic development. A disbelieving world now finds it possible to give more credence than was once fashionable to the social and economic achievements of these societies; it is still inclines to overlook or to downplay what is probably their greatest achievement — the creation of a new "spiritual economy".[76]

Jacques Decornoy has described how, in the face of the most massive air onslaught in history, the Pathet Lao are building a new educational system which integrates learning and practical work and which is helping to forge a new sense of national identity. In such a system:

> "The teacher must also be a propagandist to the people . . . Weaving, forging iron, breeding cattle, cultivating scorched fields, must hold no secrets from him".[77]

Such an integration of learning with living — and with a living which is dominated by the making of a revolution — is characteristic of North Vietnam and of the liberated zones of the South. But it is the Chinese People's Republic which offers us the most striking example of such an alternative education pattern, a pattern evolved during long years of war and civil war, tested during the reconstruction period of the 'fifties, remodelled during the Cultural Revolution, and now being tested out on a subcontinental scale. Speaking of the socialist societies of East Asia Mark Selden comments:

> "In the embryonic forms created under wartime duress are important features relevant to the future of the Third World and, indeed, to possibilities for participatory social patterns everywhere".[78]

This is especially true of the educational forms which are emerging.

In pre-Revolutionary China over four-fifths of the population was illiterate, education a privilege enjoyed by the favoured few (and used by them against the mass of their fellow-citizens), skilled technicians were rare and highly trained scientists and research workers rarer still. Under these circumstances the tasks faced by the People's Government in the educational field seemed clear: to teach the masses to read, to expand the school system to bring in as many children as rapidly as possible, to train an increasing number of skilled and semi-skilled workers and, by developing advanced education and research institutions, to greatly expand the country's resources of scientific manpower.

The progress in formal education is indicated by the fact that in 1958-59 almost 100 million students were enrolled in primary or secondary school or in institutes of higher education. The "Great Leap Forward" in 1958 brought not only a rapid increase in the numbers attending educational institutions of all kinds; it saw also the initiation of a policy of integrating education and productive work. Universities, secondary schools, and primary schools set up small factories in which pupils received technical training and which helped, if only on a small scale, to boost output figures and to defray the cost of pupils' training. At the same time, there was a rapid increase in the number of schools operated by factories, by communes, by street committees and the like. These were designed to supplement those operated by the State (they represent an application to education of the policy of "walking on two legs") and their development passed on to the community or the enterprise part of the financial burden imposed by the rapid growth in student numbers.

The integration of theory and practice, of "education" and production, was in line with Mao Tse-tung's concept of socialist education as expounded in his lecture *On Practice* as far back as 1937:

> "Knowledge begins with practice, and theoretical knowledge which is acquired through practice must then return to practice. The active function of knowledge manifests itself not only in the active leap from perceptual to rational knowledge but — and this is more important — it must manifest itself in the leap from rational knowledge to revolutionary practice".[79]

Such a philosophy not only makes it possible to break down the barriers which separate the intellectual from the worker; more positively, it gives a new reality to the learning acquired in school, since this learning can be constantly tested by the experience the student acquires in the factory or the field and enriched by the experience of the masses among whom he moves. The understanding that knowledge is of value only in so far as it can be passed on (something the Children of Barbiana recognized) begins to replace the idea of knowledge as something used to enhance one's own personal status. And the concept of a life-style of equality, in which fulfilment comes from the integration of one's intellectual and physical abilities in a common struggle, begins to create a new "spiritual economy".

And from the viewpoint of the immediate needs of a developing country such an educational policy has the immediate material advantage that the skills and competence of the student can be deployed with the minimum of delay.

Elitization — and the Cultural Revolution
By the beginning of the 1960s, then, the Chinese

educational system was beginning to develop along lines quite different from those with which the White North is familiar. Nevertheless, the dangers that education would act as a polarizing force in society were not absent; as R. F. Price commented:

"The great expansion of education . . . has been largely in the towns, and town-oriented . . . With all but a handful of the full-time secondary schools concentrated in the urban areas and the subject-matter taught concerned with urban life, these schools became a siphon drawing talent and ambition from the rural areas"[80]

Such a trend, in a still dominantly peasant society, carried with it the clear danger that education might become, as elsewhere in the developing world, a powerful force of anti-development. Even more ominous was the prospect that education, far from breaking down social barriers, might rather act as a divisive factor, leading to the emergence of an educationally-privileged élite group cut off from meaningful contact with the masses. And, as the "new classes" of the USSR and the East European People's Democracies showed, the mere establishment of a socialist system was in itself no guarantee against such a trend.

It is by reason of its confrontation of these problems that the Cultural Revolution is relevant to the whole question of education in the developing societies. For, as has been stressed earlier, such societies face not only the problem of imported (largely Western) models of economic development but, even more important, the burden of new, self-seeking, elite groups. And in China the role of these emerging elite groups was important not only in the economy but also in the political life of the country; by 1966 the CCP, which had formerly been the

⅃bodiment of the Revolution,[81] began to symbolize a pattern of behaviour and attitudes which were contradictory to the revolutionary vision. It was this budding "elitization" at the heart of society and in the Party itself which was one of the main targets of the Cultural Revolution; and, as Stephen Andors emphasises, the attack was not against the revolutionary goals of the CCP but against those in positions of authority who refused to accept that to attain these goals they had to be embodied in the concrete experience of everyday life. The Cultural Revolution firmly put "politics in command" — and "politics" in China is defined as a life style, as a specific set of human values and motivations, and as a human commitment to building a classless society free from any taint of exploitation; as such, it cannot be separate from the realities of day-to-day experience. Seen thus, the Cultural Revolution itself can be regarded as a vast and protracted process of education, involving every member of society and extended over half a decade. It was an educational process motivated by:

> "the need to create styles of leadership and forms of mass participation that will secure the economic, political, and psychological independence of the poor and exploited against élites that aim to preserve the status quo of privilege and power in all societies"[82]

And from this process there are emerging new forms of organization, new styles of education, which:

> "offer the hope of participation in planning, production, and creativity to all of their members. These organizations are based on the assumption . . . of responsibility, capability, capacity to co-operate, and the willingness to be both a teacher and a student"[83]

To a highly individual and hierarchical West,

such an assumption may appear unrealistic; decades of revolutionary struggle had, however, given Mao Tse-tung a rather different understanding of the limits of man's potential and the awareness of the extent to which this potential could be drawn out by the long and painstaking processes of education and political struggle. What the new style of education meant in practical terms was spelled out by the Central Committee of the CCP in its statement of August 1966:

"In the great proletarian cultural revolution a most important task is to transform the old educational system and the old principles and methods of teaching.

In this great cultural revolution, the phenomenon of our schools being dominated by bourgeois intellectuals must be completely changed.

In every kind of school we must apply thoroughly the policy advanced by Comrade Mao Tse-tung, of education serving proletarian politics and education being combined with productive labour so as to enable those receiving an education to develop morally, intellectually and physically and to become labourers with socialist consciousness and culture.

The period of schooling should be shortened. Courses should be fewer and better. The teaching material should be thoroughly transformed, in some cases beginning with simplifying complicated material. While their main task is to study, students should also learn other things. That is to say, in addition to their studies they should also learn industrial work, farming and military affairs, and take part in the struggles of the cultural revolution as they occur to criticize the bourgeoisie".[84]

This decision indicates the general line of development and is not a firm and detailed policy laid down by the Party; indeed, the same document states in forthright terms: "the only method is for the masses to liberate themselves, and any method of doing things on their behalf must not be used."

"A spiritual atom bomb"

Ivan Illich notes how the belief that education is something done at school and something that is very difficult and complex discourages the poor from taking over their own learning.[85] Today the Chinese are demonstrating the fallacy of this belief and showing how a whole people can take the educational process into its own hands and make of it an integral part of life itself, a means by which the vision of a Good Society is realised. All of China, says John Gurley, is "one great school".[86] There are schools run by factories and schools run by communes, there are day schools for children and evening schools for peasants, there are peasants and workers teaching in schools and universities and teachers and students who spend sizeable amounts of time working in the fields and the factories. Everywhere, experimentation and flux so that generalization is hazardous. But certain broad themes do emerge.[87]

There is the burden of the past which manifests itself in the large number of teachers moulded in the old educational system. The process of reorienting to a new and differently motivated system is slow; in the meantime the infusion of outsiders, of workers and peasants, helps speed the process of change. These help work out the general lines of development for a school, they join classes and work with teachers and students. And the composition of the group running the school — typically two or three teachers, several students, one or two workers, a member of the PLA — this ensures that education is no longer in a vacuum but that it takes account of the world outlook and "living ideas" of the students and is firmly based on proletarian politics. Class-teaching may be largely in the hands of professional teachers but they are assisted by workers, peasants, parents and the students themselves. There is the replacement of individual competition by collective effort. Students are encouraged to give lessons based on such collective work and in examination work group effort is encouraged; the object of the examinations is not to sieve out an intellectual élite but to give the students experience in the analysis of problems and a general estimate of their progress. There is the rejection of school as a ladder for individual progress and betterment; the emphasis of education is on "serving the people", on turning out students who seek not the best jobs but those that are in the interests of the people as a whole. There is an emphasis on Mao's 1966 directive about combining theory and practice and on encouraging students "to investigate for themselves, relating what is near to what is far and what is elementary to what is advanced so that the initiative of the students is stimulated". And the student should have time to "read, think, analyze, criticize and study problems".

The combination of study and practice, of schooling and productive work, has become much tighter in the last five years. Where middle schools are attached to a factory pupils put in a month a year at the factory where they and their teacher spend half the time in actual production and half in study related to this practice. At agricultural schools up to half the year is spent in productive work, either on the school's land or in the communes of the district. The majority of schools have their own small workshop or factory and work here is regarded as complementary to the work-period spent by pupils in the bigger factory. The latter gives the students an opportunity to learn something of the realities of society and industry from the workers but, quite obviously, the operation of the factory cannot readily be halted to give technical instruction (see above, p. 59 on the need for redesigning the industrial process) so the pupils have their own machines in the school; these are often old and in converting and modernizing them the pupils gain valuable experience and a sense of self-reliance. This pattern extends, as we have seen, to the agriculture sector.[88] Such developments are important not only because they eliminate the gap between theory and practice or the division between student and worker but because they go far to making the whole educational process a self-supporting process; they thus help to solve the biggest and most basic problem faced by orthodox systems of education — that these orthodox systems are simply not economically viable, given the poverty of most emerging nations. And by drawing the workers into the schools so that technical skills and experience can be passed on to the pupils the Chinese system conforms to the ideal of the children of Barbiana — that "knowledge is only meant to be passed on".

The pattern we have described is a fluid pattern for, as the Chinese see it, rules or programmes are not made for all time, but the trend is clear and it is a trend which, by liberating the latent potential of young and old, is fashioning that "spiritual atom bomb" of human energy and human creativity of which Mao has spoken. Indeed, in this respect, the Chinese reshaping of their educational system is of greater world significance than China's emergence as a nuclear power or the dramatic transformation of her physical environment.[89]

China is in a ferment — of learning, teaching, inventing. But, as Joseph Needham points out, millions of those who have been caught up in this ferment are folk who have had little education of any sort, who need guidance on how to think, on how to set about the analysis of the practical problems with which they are grappling. Consequently, in the last year or so increasing attention has been given to this and philosophy classes have sprung up in the factories and on the communes, designed to show how Mao's dialectical philosophy can help folk think about the contradictions and the problems they meet in their day-to-day work. Says Joseph Needham:

> "Everything's full of paradoxes, problems and difficulties. Everybody faces this in all countries, but with some guidance on how to think, the problems can be solved. The Chinese people are being encouraged tremendously now to do this"[90]

One final aspect of the Chinese experiment is the elaboration of what Needham terms "a new moral theology". Among the major stumbling blocks to progress in the Third World is, we have seen, the selfishness and materialism of those shaped by the imported educational system of the White North. Education in China, by contrast, sets itself the objective of eradicating privilege, selfishness, self-interest — in short, of eradicating all those "qualities" on which conventional education relies for motivation. The Chinese recognise, quite simply, that the objective construction of a new society, a real socialist society, is irrelevant unless the necessity for subjective change, for an inner conversion, is first recognized. The target of revolution, and of the education which is an inseparable part of the revolutionary process, is thus not merely other people but the weaknesses and failings in oneself. And in this emphasis on the need for inner conversion, this faith in the perfectibility of man and of all men, and in this vision of a Good Society some

71

detect striking parallels with the vision of those who shaped Galilean Christianity . . .[91] At the very least there is sufficient to make us pause before accepting Robert M. Hutchin's confident assertion that the Chinese "are interested only in scientific, technical, and industrial achievement".[92]

Education — "for all whose fate it is to be born human beings"

As the economies of the Third World have been warped by the impact of the White North so too have its educational systems. There is, therefore, a certain irony in the belief widely held in the "director societies" (as Freire terms the societies of the White North) that in both the economic and educational fields, indeed, in almost any field one may mention, progress in the Third World is inconceivable without "aid" from the North, without adopting the patterns of development which the North itself followed. The view can be challenged on many grounds but its ultimate unreality is evident when its financial implications are examined. We have compared the educational systems of the North to a white elephant, to the gift whose upkeep is ruinous to its recipient. Yet is such a situation simply to be dismissed as "ironical" — or is it not rather the result of cold and careful planning by the "director societies"? As Paolo Freire remarks: " 'salvation' of the Third World by the director societies can only mean its domination", and if there are those who:

> "study all the possibilities which the future contains (it is) in order to 'domesticate' it and keep it in line with the present, which is what they intend to maintain"[93]

In such domination and domestication a key role

is played by the "Brown Sahibs", the new élites whom the White North has fashioned. Such groups lack authenticity as far as the masses of their country are concerned and, lacking authenticity, are highly vulnerable to popular discontent and disenchantment; maintenance of their position demands therefore a rigid and authoritarian structure. Such power élites are "silent in the face of the metropolis, (and they) silence their own people in turn".[94] Some two-thirds of humankind are imprisoned within this "culture of silence" and this is no historical accident, rather does this division of our human world into "men" and "less-than-men" arise from the structural relations between the director societies and their dependent societies. And given this there is little hope of real educational progress in the Third World in the schemes and the aid proffered by those "who intend to make the future repeat their present"; rather does the only hope lie in the breaking of the old structures which have brought dependence and domination. It is in their demonstration of this truth that the importance of the East Asian socialist societies lies and this is nowhere more evident than in the field of education.

These societies, and especially the Chinese People's Republic, are attempting to translate into reality ideals of education which are strikingly similar to those expressed by Comenius four centuries ago:

> "Our first wish is that all men should be educated fully to full humanity; not any one individual, nor a few nor even many, but all men together and singly, young and old, rich and poor, of high and lowly birth, men and women — in a word all whose fate it is to be born human beings . . .
>
> Our second wish is that every man should be wholly educated,

rightly formed not only in one single matter or in a few or even in many, but in all things which perfect human nature . . ."[95]

Such a policy means an end to élites and to privilege. It stands opposed to that "social irrationality"[96] born of specialisation which is the bane of the overdeveloped societies. It eschews the common idea that the people are incapable of knowing and action and it "invites the people to grasp with their minds the truth of their reality."[97] It recognizes that any literacy programme, any education system, must, in Freire's words, "relate *speaking the word* to *transforming reality* and to man's role in this transformation" (emphasis in original). Above all, it sees education as a process in which men — all men — learn to move with increasing self-confidence to the rejection of all forms of manipulation, whether by other societies or élite groups within their own society, and, liberated, begin "to add to the life they have the existence they themselves make". And this growing process of "conscientization", involving over a fifth of mankind, marks the beginning of a new epoch of human history . . .[98]

KEITH BUCHANAN

REFERENCES

1. Gerald Hanley, *The Drinkers of Darkness* (London, 1960), pp. 16-17.

2. *New Left Review* (London), Jan-Feb 1963, p. 4.

3. Nguyen Huu Chau, "Les coûts de l'éducation" in *Tiers-Monde* (Paris), April-June 1965, p. 426.

4. Martin Carnoy, "Schooling and Income" in *Pacific Research and World Empire Telegram* (East Palo Alto), July-August 1971, p. 2.

5. See C. R. Hensman, *From Gandhi to Guevara* (London, 1969).

6. Rick Greenspan, "Secondary Education: The Corporations Move In" in *Pacific Research and World Empire Telegram,* Nov. 1970, pp. 10-16.

7. Tarzie Vittachi, *The Brown Sahibs* (London, 1962), p. 9. For a discussion of élites see Javier Prats Llauradó "Elites without elitism" in *Ceres* (FAO) May-June 1971.

8. See, on this, the Encyclicals of Popes John XXIII (notably *Peace on Earth,* 1963) and Paul VI (notably *The Great Social Problem,* 1967).

9. Jerome Rothenberg, *Technicians of the Sacred* quoted in *Nation,* 28 July 1969, p. 86.

10. Robin Flower, *The Irish Tradition* (Oxford, 1966 edition), pp. 104-106.

11. UNESCO (Paris, 1957).

12. Quoted in *I. F. Stone's Bi-weekly,* 24 February 1969, p. 3.

13. Frederick Harbison and Charles A. Myers, *Education, Manpower and Economic Growth* (New York and London, 1964), pp. 31-32.

14. *ibid.,* p. 33.

15. See, for example, Paul Bairoch, *Diagnostic de l'évolution économique du Tiers-Monde 1900-1966* (Paris, 1967); Pierre Jalée, *Le tiers-monde dans l'économie mondiale* (Paris, 1968); Jacques Freyssinet, *Le concept de sous-développement* (Paris and La Haye, 1966).

16. Paul Bairoch, *op. cit.,* p. 171.

17. Jacques Freyssinet, *op. cit.,* p. 26.

18. *ibid.* On the relationship between technical training and resource development in Africa see Jean-Pierre N'Diaye "The problem is vision" in *Ceres* (FAO) July-Aug. 1973.

19. René Gendarme, *La pauvreté des nations* (Paris, 1963), p. 473.

20. *ibid.*

21. cited by René Gendarme, *op. cit.*, p. 478.

22. Netherlands Economic Institute, "Financial Aspects of the Educational Expansion in Developing Regions" in *The World Yearbook on Education 19* (London), p. 71.

23. The School of Barbiana, *Letter to a Teacher* translated by Nora Rossi and Tom Cole (Harmondsworth, 1970), pp. 35, 90.

24. Rémi Van Waeyenberghe, "L'école et l'enfant dans les pays du Tiers Monde" in *Les carnets de l'enfance/Assignment Children* (Unicef, Paris), January 1968, pp. 38-51. See also Gabriel Carceles Breis "Stark Profile of Wastage in Education" in *Courier* (UNESCO) June 1972.

25. *ibid.*, p. 51.

26. See, on this, Andrew Péarse ". . . with good intentions" in *Ceres* (FAO) May-June 1971.

27. Paul Goodman, *Growing Up Absurd* (London, 1970 edition), p. 175.

28. cited by Madeleine Trébous in "La civilisation africaine face à l'occident" in *Développement et Civilisations* (Paris), Oct-Dec 1962, p. 103.

29. Peter Worsley in *Out of Apathy* ed. E. P. Thompson (London, 1960), p. 139.

30. Robert Heilbroner, *The Great Ascent* (New York, 1963), p. 24.

31. Martin Carnoy, *op. cit.*, p. 2.

32. C. R. Hensman, *Rich against Poor: The Reality of Aid* (London, 1971), p. 78.

33. Renato Constantino, "The Mis-Education of the Filipino" in *Journal of Contemporary Asia,* Autumn 1970, p. 26.

34. Frederick Harbison and Charles A. Myers, op. cit., p. 85.

35. Ivan Illich, "Outwitting the 'Developed' Countries" in *New York Review of Books,* 6 November 1969.

36. Ivan Illich, "The Futility of Schooling in Latin America" in *Saturday Review,* 20 April 1968, p. 74.

37. Ivan Illich, "Schooling: The Ritual of Progress" in *N. York Review of Books,* 3 December 1970. p. 20.

38. Jacques Berque, "Vers une humanité plénière" in *Esprit* (Paris). April 1969, p. 653.

39. Professor H. J. Paton, discussing education, comments on "the English benevolence which is determined to share its own unachieved — ideals with other people whether they want to have them or not". *The Claim of Scotland* (London, 1968), p. 251. And, for a more recent critique of "Western" education see Edward Goldsmith "Education: For What?" in *The Ecologist* (London) Jan. 1974.

40. See the work by Tarzie Vittachi cited above and also Nirad C. Chaudhuri, *The Continent of Circe* (London, 1965).

41. Preface to Franz Fanon, *The Wretched of the Earth* (Penguin, 1967), p. 7.

42. Richard Harris, *Independence and After* (London, 1962), p. 13. Robert McDonald, in his article "The Arrogance of Ability", suggests "the mass-distribution to student leaders in the developed countries (both Western and Communist) of the works of Franz Fanon". *The New African,* December 1966.

43. Pierre van den Bergh, "European Languages and Black Mandarins" in *Transition* (Dar-es-Salaam), Dec-Jan 1968, p. 19.

44. Renato Constantino, *op. sup. cit.,* p. 24. See also Pierre van den Berghe, *op. cit.,* p. 20.

45. Pierre van den Berghe, *op. cit.* This generalisation is far less relevant in the case of Latin American students than in the case of African students.

46. See Clemente Chirinos, "L'attitude des dirigeants de jeunes nations face aux problèmes de développement" in *Développement et Civilisations* Jan-March 1962, pp. 65-70.

47. Ivan Illich, "Schooling: the Ritual of Progress", *op. sup. cit.,* p. 20.

48. Philip Altbach, "Neocolonialism and Education: Some Facts" in *United Asia,* May-June 1970, p. 153.

49. Quoted in *The Philippine Collegian* (Quezon City), 6 March 1959, p. 4.

50. Cited by W. G. Archer, *India and Modern Art* (London, 1959), p. 19.

51. On "academic objectivity" see, for example, Robert Engler, "Social Science and Social Consciousness" in *The Dissenting Academy* ed. Theodore Roszak (New York 1967) and Noam Chomsky, *American Power and the New Mandarins* (Penguin, 1969).

52. Rick Greenspan, *op. sup. cit.,* p. 10.

53. Africa Research Group, *Africa Retort* (Cambridge, 1970), pp. 70-71.

54. *ibid.,* p. 69.

55. Gary McEoin in *National Catholic Reporter,* June 12, 1970, p. 11; see also Claude Julien, *L'empire américain* (Paris, 1968).

56. Malayang Pagkakaisa Ng Kabataang Pilipino (MPKP), *Peoples Power* (no date) pp. 8, 6.

57. School of Barbiana, *Letter to a Teacher* (Penguin Education Special, 1970).

58. Brian Jackson & Dennis Marsden, *Education and the Working Class* (New York, 1962), p. 192.

59. See for example Herbert Kohl, *36 Children* (London, 1968) and Jonathan Kozol, *Death at an early age* (Penguin Education Special, 1968).

60. Suburban newspaper quoted in *The Hornsey Affair* by Students and Staff of Hornsey College of Art, (Penguin Education Special, 1969).

61. Padraic H. Pearse, "The Murder Machine" in *Collected Works* (Dublin & London, 1922) especially pp. 6-7.

62. Paul Goodman, *Growing up Absurd* (Sphere Books, London, 1970) p. 22.

63. Denis Goulet, "The Disappointing Decade of Development" in *The Center Magazine,* September 1969, p. 63.

64. *The Great Social Problem,* para. 14.

65. C. R. Hensman, *"Rich against Poor . . .",* p. 78.

66. See, for example, Edward Blishen (ed.) *The School that I'd like* (Penguin, 1969), R. F. Mackenzie, *State School* (Penguin, 1970), David Rubinstein and Colin Stoneman (ed.) *Education for Democracy* (Penguin, 1970).

67. Frederick Harbison and Charles A. Myers, *op. cit.,* p. 128. Adam Curle notes that: "In Ghana . . . a primary school teacher is paid four times more relative to the national average income than one in the USA". "Some Aspects of Educational Planning in Underdeveloped Areas" in *Harvard Educational Review,* Summer 1962, p. 297.

68. cf. John Tripp:
   ". . . who loves not his own patch
   of plundered soil, learns nothing of pity for all men"
   Poetry Wales, Spring 1969.

69. See references under 59 above and Students and Staff of Hornsey College of Art (ed.) *The Hornsey Affair,* Brian Jackson and Denis Marsden, *Education and the Working Class* (New York, 1962), Herbert Kohl, *36 Children* (London, 1968) and Jonathan Kozol, *Death at an Early Age* (Penguin, 1968).

70. Paolo Freire, "The Adult Literacy Process as Cultural Action for Freedom" in *Harvard Educational Review,* May and August 1970; Ivan Illich: see footnotes 34-36 above. Also Paolo Freire, *Pedagogy of the Oppressed* (New York, 1970) and Ivan Illich, *De-schooling Society* (London & New York 1971).

71. Ivan Illich, "Why We Must Abolish Schooling", p. 11.

72. *ibid.,* p. 10.

73. Ivan Illich, "The Futility of Schooling", p. 75.

74. *ibid.*

75. Paolo Freire, *op. sup. cit.*, May 1970, p. 205.

76. Neale Hunter, "The Good Earth and the Good Society" in *China and Ourselves,* ed. Bruce Douglass and Ross Terrill (Boston, 1970), pp. 183-185.

77. Jacques Decornoy, "Laos: The Forgotten War" in *Bulletin of Concerned Asian Scholars,* April/ July 1970, pp. 26-27.

78. Mark Selden, "Peoples War and the Transformation of Peasant Society" in Edward Friedman and Mark Selden (ed.) *America's Asia* (New York, 1971), p. 361. Also Mark Selden *The Yenan Way in Revolutionary China* (Camb, Mass. 1971) esp pp. 267-274 & *passim.*

79. Quotations from Chairman Mao Tse-tung (Peking, 1966), pp. 209-10.

80. R. F. Price, "China — In Search of an Anti-City Education" in *The World Yearbook of Education 196* (London), pp. 36-37.

81. Much of this paragraph is based on Stephen Andors, "Revolution and Modernization: Man and Machine in Industrializing Societies, the Chinese Case" in *America's Asia,* pp. 393 sqq.

82. Stephen Andors, *op. cit.*, p. 395.

83. *ibid.*, pp. 436-37.

84. Text given in full in *Peking Review,* 12 August 1966, p. 8.

85. Ivan Illich, "Why We Must Abolish Schooling", p. 10.

86. John G. Gurley, "Capitalist and Maoist Economic Development" in *America's Asia,* p. 346.

87. The following paragraph is based largely on Roland Berger, "Education in China" in *China Now* (London), July 1970; see also Patrick Daly, "A new way to learning" in *China Now,* January 1971 and Ilsa Sharp, "No Ivory Towers" in *Far Eastern Economic Review,* June 5, 1971, pp. 64-66.

88. Examples of part-work, part-study schools are given in Keith Buchanan, *The Transformation of the Chinese Earth* (London, 1970), pp. 303-305.

89. *ibid.*

90. Joseph Needham, "The alchemy of human nature" in *China Now,* January 1971, p. 6; see also "Peasants and Philosophy" in *Eastern Horizon* (Hong Kong), Volume X, Number 3 (1971), pp. 8-20.

91. See Neale Hunter, "The Good Earth . . ." and the essays by Ray Wylie, Kazuhiko Sumiya, and Bruce Douglass in the volume cited.

92. Robert M. Hutchins, *The Learning Society* (London, 1968), p. 63.

93. Paolo Freire, *op. sup. cit.*, May 1970, pp. 220-221.

94. *idem.*, August 1970, p. 459.

95. *The Great Didactic* cited in Robert M. Hutchins, *op. cit.*, p. viii.

96. John MacDermott, "Technology: The Opiate of the Intellectuals" in *New York Review of Books*, 31 July 1969, p. 31.

97. Paolo Freire, *op. cit.*, August 1970, p. 477.

98. Paolo Freire defines "conscientization" as "the process in which men, not as recipients, but as knowing subjects, achieve a deepening awareness both of the socio-cultural reality which shapes their lives and of their capacity to transform that reality". See Paolo Freire *op. sup. cit.* and his discussion of extension work in "Knowledge is a critical appraisal of the World" *Ceres* (FAO) May-June 1971.